JOURNAL

205
Ruled
Pages

COSCOM ENTERAINMENT
WINNIPEG

This is a journal. Would be silly to put a copyright disclaimer here now, wouldn't it, especially since the content is yours? - APF

ISBN 978-1-927339-99-2

Published by Coscom Entertainment

Printed and bound in the USA

Cover art and design by A.P. Fuchs

~

This Journal Belongs
to

~

_____

~

~

~

~

~

~

~

~

~

~

~

~

www.apfuchs.ca